The True Costs
of Prisons

Series Titles

- **The History of Punishment and Imprisonment**
- **Juveniles Growing Up in Prison**
- **Political Prisoners**
- **Prison Alternatives and Rehabilitation**
- **Prison Conditions Around the World**
- **The Treatment of Prisoners and Prison Conditions**
- **The True Cost of Prisons**
- **Unequal Justice**
- **Women Incarcerated**

The True Cost of Prisons

BY **Autumn Libal**

FOREWORD BY **Larry E. Sullivan, PhD**

Associate Dean, John Jay College of Criminal Justice

MASON CREST

Mason Crest
450 Parkway Drive, Suite D
Broomall, PA 19008
www.masoncrest.com

Printed and bound in the United States of America.

First printing
9 8 7 6 5 4 3 2 1

Series ISBN: 978-1-4222-3781-6
Hardcover ISBN: 978-1-4222-3788-5
ebook ISBN: 978-1-4222-8003-4

Library of Congress Cataloging-in-Publication Data

Names: Libal, Autumn, author.
Title: The true costs of prisons / by Autumn Libal ; foreword by Larry E. Sullivan, PhD, Associate Dean, John Jay College of Criminal Justice.
Other titles: Social, monetary, and moral costs of prisons
Description: Broomall, PA : Mason Crest, [2018] | Series: The prison system | Includes index.
Identifiers: LCCN 2016054098| ISBN 9781422237885 (hardback) | ISBN 9781422237816 (series) | ISBN 9781422280034 (ebook)
Subjects: LCSH: Prisons--United States--Costs--Juvenile literature. | Prisons--North America--Costs--Juvenile literature. | Imprisonment--Moral and ethical aspects--Juvenile literature.
Classification: LCC HV9471 .L53 2018 | DDC 365/.973--dc23

Developed and Produced by Print Matters Productions, Inc.
(www.printmattersinc.com)

Cover and Interior Design: Tom Carling, Carling Design
Additional Text: Brian Boone

Contents

Foreword by Larry E. Sullivan, PhD 6

1 What Prisons Have to Do with You 9

2 The Prison Population of the United States 19

3 The Monetary Costs 27

4 The Social Costs 41

5 The Moral Costs 59

6 Need for Prison Reform? 67

Series Glossary 75

Further Resources 78

Index 79

About the Author, Series Consultant, and Picture Credits..............80

KEY ICONS TO LOOK FOR:

Words to understand: These words with their easy-to-understand definitions will increase the reader's understanding of the text while building vocabulary skills.

Sidebars: This boxed material within the main text allows readers to build knowledge, gain insights, explore possibilities, and broaden their perspectives by weaving together additional information to provide realistic and holistic perspectives.

Educational Videos: Readers can view videos by scanning our QR codes, providing them with additional educational content to supplement the text. Examples include news coverage, moments in history, speeches, iconic sports moments and much more!

Text-dependent questions: These questions send the reader back to the text for more careful attention to the evidence presented there.

Research projects: Readers are pointed toward areas of further inquiry connected to each chapter. Suggestions are provided for projects that encourage deeper research and analysis.

Series glossary of key terms: This back-of-the-book glossary contains terminology used throughout this series. Words found here increase the reader's ability to read and comprehend higher-level books and articles in this field.

Foreword

Prisons have a long history, one that began with the idea of evil, guilt, and atonement. In fact, the motto of one of the first prison reform organizations was "Sin no more." Placing offenders in prison was, for most of the history of prison systems, a ritual for redemption through incarceration; hence the language of punishment takes on a very religious cast. The word *penitentiary* itself comes from the concept of penance, or self-punishment to make up for a past wrong. When we discuss prisons, we are dealing not only with the law, but with very strong emotions and reactions to acts that range from minor crimes, or misdemeanors, to major crimes, or felonies, such as murder and rape.

Prisons also reflect the level of the civilizing process through which a culture travels, and it tells us much about how we treat our fellow human beings. The 19th-century Russian author Fyodor Dostoyevsky, who was a political prisoner, remarked, "The degree of civilization in a society can be measured by observing its prisoners." Similarly, Winston Churchill, the British prime minister during World War II, said that the "treatment of crime and criminals is one of the most unfailing tests of civilization of any country."

For much of the history of the American prison, we tried to rehabilitate or modify the criminal behavior of offenders through a variety of treatment programs. In the last quarter of the 20th century, politicians and citizens alike realized that this attempt had failed, and they began passing stricter laws, imprisoning people for longer terms, and building more prisons. This movement has taken a great toll on society. Beginning in the 1970s federal and state governments passed mandatory minimum sentencing laws, stricter habitual offender legislation, and other "tough on crime" laws that have led today to the incarceration in prisons and jails of approximately 2.3 million people, or an imprisonment rate of 720 per 100,000 people, the highest recorded level in the world. This has led to the overcrowding of prisons, worse living conditions, fewer educational programs, and severe budgetary problems. Imprisonment carries a significant social cost since it splits families and contributes to a cycle of crime, violence, drug addiction, and poverty. The Federal Sentencing Reform Act of 1984 created a grid of offenses and crime categories for sentencing that disallowed mitigating circumstances. This grid was meant to prevent disparate sentences for similar crimes. The government made these guidelines mandatory, thereby taking most discretionary sentencing out of the hands of judges who previously could give a wider range of sentences, such as one year to life, and allow for some type of rehabilitation. The unintended consequences of this legislative reform in sentencing was the doubling of the number of incarcerated people in the United States. Combined with the harsh sentences on drug offenders, almost half of the prisoners in the federal system are narcotics offenders, both violent and nonviolent, traffickers and users. States followed suit in enacting the harsh guidelines of the federal government in sentencing patterns. "Life without parole" laws and the changes in parole and probation practices led to even more offenders behind bars. Following the increase in the number of incarcerated offenders, more and more prisons were built with the aid of federal funds and filled to the brim with both violent and nonviolent offenders. In addition,

many states handed over penal custody to the new private for-profit prisons that stemmed from mass incarceration.

In the 21st century officials, politicians, and the public began to realize that such drastic laws wrought much harm to society. With the spread of long-term imprisonment, those who had spent decades in prison were unemployable after release. Their criminal histories followed them and made it difficult if not impossible to find gainful employment. Therefore, they entered the criminal world continually and thus sped up the vicious cycle of crime-imprisonment-release-crime-punishment. America was reaching the tipping point; something had to give.

In response to this growing trend of harsh sentencing, for example, the Supreme Court led the way between 2005 and 2016 with decisions banning the death penalty for juveniles (Roper v. Simmons, U.S. 551 [2005]), life sentence without parole for juveniles not convicted of homicide (Graham v. Florida, 130 S. Ct. 2011 [2010]); and life without parole for juveniles (Miller v. Alabama and Jackson v. Hobbes 132 S. Ct. 2455 [2012] and Montgomery v. Louisiana 135 S.Ct. 1729 [2015]). Behavioral psychologists and other officials do not consider juveniles capable of making fully formed decisions, and the Supreme Court has recognized the developmental differences that excuses full individual responsibility and applies to their actions the philosophic principle of just deserts. Many states (90 percent of prisoners are under state, not federal jurisdiction) are beginning to take action by reducing harsh mandatory sentences for adults. Most states, for example, have gone toward the decriminalization or legalization of marijuana, with lighter penalties for possession of the drug. Since most prisoners in state institutions are violent, however, contemporary America is caught in a dilemma with which many academics and governmental policy makers are aggressively grappling.

All these are reasons why this series on the prison system is extremely important for understanding the history and culture of the United States. Readers will learn all facets of punishment: its history; the attempts to rehabilitate offenders; the increasing number of women and juveniles in prison; the inequality of sentencing among the races; attempts to find alternatives to incarceration; the high cost, both economically and morally, of imprisonment; and other equally important issues. These books teach us the importance of understanding that the prison system affects more people in the United States than any institution, other than our schools.

LARRY E. SULLIVAN, PHD
Associate Dean
Chief Librarian
John Jay College of Criminal Justice
Professor of Criminal Justice
Graduate School and University Center
City University of New York

1 What Prisons Have to Do with You

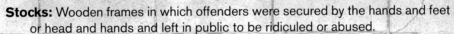

Words to Understand

Punitive: Inflicting or intended to punish.

Stocks: Wooden frames in which offenders were secured by the hands and feet or head and hands and left in public to be ridiculed or abused.

Vindictive: Characterized by a desire to hurt somebody.

Most people have never been in trouble with the law, and many people have never known someone who has been to prison. In fact, most people in the United States go about their daily lives rarely thinking about prisons. A crime-related news story may catch our attention, or a corrections facility sign might catch our eye. But for the most part, prisons and prison issues are not even a blip on our radar screens. So you might think prisons have nothing to do with your life.

Ignoring prisons as a relevant part of all of our lives, however, overlooks a basic fact. The incarceration system is an integral part of how American society runs, and everyone has a stake in that system functioning effectively.

All societies are based on sets of rules their members generally choose to obey. Those rules can come in many forms, from voluntary social graces, like saying

Many of us are not used to the sight of a prison cell; however, the prison system affects our lives every day.

please and thank you, to official laws, like bans on littering and the prohibition of many drugs. When members of a society follow the rules, which most members do without even thinking about it, society runs smoothly. When people break the rules, society can suffer a breakdown.

Inevitably, even mandatory rules are broken, sometimes in minor ways—like a child stealing bubble gum from a corner store—and sometimes in major ways—like gang members committing murder in a drive-by shooting. For the good of the whole, societies must decide how to deal with individuals who threaten the harmony of the social order by breaking mandatory laws. To deal with the perpetrators of crime, most societies develop penal systems—systems of punishment. The more severe the crime is, the more drastic the punishment.

Most societies around the world have developed penal systems that rely on methods of incarceration to deal with those who break laws. The United States is no exception. In fact, the incarceration system as it currently exists in much of the world was developed in America, and to this day it is North America's number-one method of dealing with people who commit serious crimes.

What Our Addiction to Prison Costs

The money America spends on prisons means less money for other things.

Prisons as a More Humane Punishment

The incarceration system that operates in North America and much of the world today has its roots in the late 1600s in Pennsylvania. There, the Quakers, a religious group defined by a deep commitment to peace, began developing incarceration as a humane alternative to the punishment system of the time, which was defined by corporal punishment—punishment of the body, such as whipping or confinement in **stocks**—and capital punishment—punishment by death. Before this time, people were generally only held in jails while they awaited their sentencing; jail itself was not the punishment. The Quakers and others experimenting with the idea of imprisonment as a punishment in itself saw incarceration as an ethical alternative to what they viewed as morally repugnant sentences of the day.

Although the first experiments began in the late 1600s, America's incarceration movement didn't really take hold until more than a hundred years later. In the early 1800s, the first great social experiments in imprisonment began, most notably in Philadelphia, PA, and Auburn, NY. The focus of these institutions was meant to be reform; prisoners were to lead a life of isolation, religious contemplation, and physical labor. Through these means, it was believed the individual would be reborn and would emerge from prison as a hardworking, law-abiding Christian.

Within mere decades, the idealism and optimism that had fueled the great prison experiments had all but disappeared. Prisons were dank, overcrowded human warehouses where forced labor and corporal punishment once again ruled. Whippings, stocks, cold-water baths—all things that prisons were supposed to eliminate—were now frequently used as punishment for misbehavior within prison walls.

In the United States, there have always been large social, cultural, and economic differences between the industrial North and the agricultural South. These differences affected the regional evolution of prisons. In the North, prisons became industrial institutions where prisoners labored producing goods—prison factories. In the South, they became agricultural institutions where prisoners labored in the fields—prison farms.

Prisons Evolve

In 1870, the National Prison Association formed. In its opening congress, the association spoke out against the trends that had developed in American prisons stating, "Reformation, not **vindictive** suffering, should be the purpose of penal treatment of prisoners." Thus a new age of prison reform began, and prisons continue to evolve and change today.

Throughout their evolution, prisons have steadily moved from punishment of the body to punishment of the mind. Today, our society views the harshest penalty of prison to be the individual's loss of freedom. Even within prison walls, varying levels of rights and freedoms have replaced physical punishments for misbehavior. Inmates who behave well earn greater freedoms—privileges like recreation, time spent in the prison library (if there is one), and the ability to see visitors. Inmates who misbehave have their few freedoms taken away; they have privileges like recreation removed, get "keeplocked" (confined to their cells), or are placed in solitary confinement.

This movement from punishment of the body to punishment of the mind is, in many ways, far more humane than the corporal and capital punishments that were the norm before the incarceration system was developed. That does not, however, mean that today's incarceration system is without problems, ethical and moral challenges, and negative costs and consequences. The degree of these problems, challenges, and consequences is directly related to how well an incarceration system is fulfilling its role or function in a society.

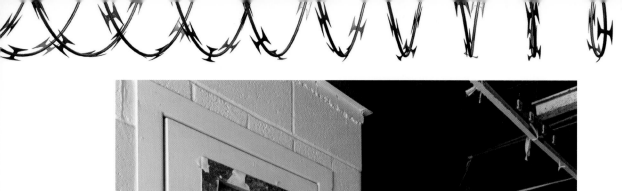

Solitary confinement cells at the West Virginia State Penitentiary.

The Role of Prisons in Society

Incarceration clearly has an important role to play in society—it is the method by which perpetrators of crime are punished. But punishment is not the only purpose of the incarceration system. The incarceration system is also meant to serve a protective purpose—it is meant to protect law-abiding citizens by separating dangerous criminals from the rest of the population and confining them where they cannot harm others. Deterrence is another important function incarceration is intended to serve; the existence of the system—the mere threat of losing one's freedom—is supposed to deter people from committing crimes in the first place. Ideally, incarceration is also meant to serve an additional purpose, this one rehabilitative. Most prisoners will serve out their term, be released from prison, and reenter the rest of the population. In an ideal system, prisoners would receive the necessary care, training, and resources to reform their behavior, ensuring that once released from prison they will not continue a life of crime.

Federal Bureau of Prisons Mission Statement

It is the mission of the Federal Bureau of Prisons to protect society by confining offenders in the controlled environments of prisons and community-based facilities that are safe, humane, cost-efficient, and appropriately secure, and that provide work and other self-improvement opportunities to assist offenders in becoming law-abiding citizens.

(From the Federal Bureau of Prisons website.)

The Federal Bureau of Prisons Seal.

Some prisons allow prisoners access to education.

Incarceration systems in North America today face many challenges. In the United States, the focus of the prison system is clearly and overwhelmingly punitive—it serves above all to punish people for their crimes. How well, however, the system fulfills its deterrence, protective, and rehabilitative functions is an issue of great debate. In Canada, the incarceration system is structured very similarly to that in the United States. However, it has important differences as well, and in general Canada's system is more focused on rehabilitation than the U.S. system is. Michael Jacobson, former commissioner of the New York City Corrections Commission and a professor of criminology at John Jay Law School in New York City, describes the differences between the systems this way: "Canadian corrections are generally much more into rehabilitation in prisons and reentry. They're not as punishment-oriented as we are. There is an emphasis on dealing with the underlying issues."

The Hidden Costs of Prisons

Every incarceration system, whether its focus is **punitive**, protective, rehabilitative, or other, has costs associated with it. These costs range from the straightforward and easily quantifiable monetary costs of running the facilities, to the more complicated social and moral costs associated with prisons' larger effects on individuals and society. When the costs of incarceration systems are not properly understood and addressed, they spill out into the larger society with complicated and unexpected negative consequences. Such negative consequences threaten to weaken government budgets, families, communities, the social order, and public safety. The greater a society's understanding of the monetary, social, and moral costs of its incarceration system, the better equipped that society will be to develop a cost-efficient, effective, just, and humane system that not only houses criminals but also ultimately makes all of society stronger and safer.

Developing a financially and ethically sound incarceration system, however, is no easy task; incarceration has been used as punishment for hundreds of years, yet debates about how to improve this penal system continue. These debates are sure to continue for years to come, for the actions societies take to deal with people who commit crimes raise some of the most profound questions and dilemmas human civilization faces. When dealing with perpetrators of crime, those in charge of meting out justice must decide how action can be taken against these individuals that effectively and justly deals with the crimes committed, while still acknowledging and properly treating the humanity of everyone involved.

Text-Dependent Questions

1. What religious group created the first American prisons, and when?
2. Prisons were initially created as an alternative to what kinds of punishment?
3. What was the goal of the National Prison Association when it formed?

Research Projects

1. Research the history of prisons in another developed nation. What are some ways that they have changed over time?
2. What are some of the fundamental differences between American and Canadian prisons?

2 The Prison Population of the United States

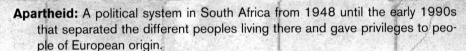

Words to Understand

Apartheid: A political system in South Africa from 1948 until the early 1990s that separated the different peoples living there and gave privileges to people of European origin.

Industrialized: Adapted to industrial methods of production and manufacturing.

Public-order crimes: Victimless crimes, such as prostitution.

The first step in discerning the costs and consequences of America's incarceration systems is to understand its scope: the structures, the people it affects, and how it is run. In the United States, the incarceration system is overseen by three levels of government: local, state, and federal. On the local level, inmates are incarcerated in jails. On the state and federal levels, inmates are incarcerated in state or federal prisons. Currently, the United States has 5,104 adult incarceration establishments: 3,283 of these are local jails, 1,719 are state facilities, and 102 are federal facilities.

According to the U.S. Bureau of Justice Statistics, there are more than 2.3 million people incarcerated in the United States. This means that, nationwide, one in every 138 people is incarcerated—a shockingly high number. In fact, it's the highest incarceration rate anywhere in the world—approximately seven times higher than in Canada.

The guard tower at Louisiana's maximum security Angola prison.

The World's Leader in Incarceration

As the world's incarceration leader, the United States has far more people who have served time behind bars than the 2.3 million currently in prison. According to the Bureau of Justice Statistics, approximately 7.2 million adults have been incarcerated in a U.S. state or federal prison. And these numbers don't even include the people who have ever spent time held in a local jail. When one begins to total all the past inmates, the number of people in the United States who have personally experienced life behind bars swells to a significant percentage of the population. As of 2010, one in every 33 adult U.S. residents had spent time in a state or federal prison at some point in their life. But someday, this could be just the tip of the "prisoner iceberg." The U.S. Bureau of Justice Statistics predicts that, if recent incarceration rates remain unchanged, an estimated 1 out of every 15 persons in the United States will serve time in a prison at some point in his or her lifetime.

The United States, however, was not always the world's leader in incarceration. Throughout the 20th century, the United States had relatively high incarceration rates compared to other Western, **industrialized** countries, but those rates were still low compared to countries with more severe penal systems, such as **apartheid** South Africa and communist Russia. In the last 25 years, however, imprisonment has soared in the United States, jettisoning the nation into its now infamous position as the world's incarceration leader.

According to the U.S. Federal Bureau of Prisons, from 1980 to 1989, the [federal] inmate population more than doubled, from just over 24,000 to almost 58,000. During the 1990s, the population more than doubled again, reaching approximately 136,000 at the end of 1999 as efforts to combat illegal drugs and illegal immigration contributed to significantly increased conviction rates.

Today, the number of federal prison inmates is more than 1.5 million prisoners. State prisons have experienced a similar swelling to the doubling and then redoubling that the federal prisons have experienced.

Why Does the U.S. Jail So Many People?

How and why the United States' criminal justice system became the largest in the world.

Poverty and Lack of Education Are Behind the Prison Profile

The numbers presented by the U.S. Bureau of Justice Statistics, however, reveal that rates of imprisonment are by no means equal throughout the U.S. population. It is not, in fact, 1 out of *every* 33 adults nationwide who is likely to be incarcerated. A person's chances of being incarcerated are greatly affected by race, ethnicity, and gender. The prevalence of imprisonment is much higher for black and Hispanic males than for white males. In fact, combined state and federal incarceration rates are approximately five times higher for black males and twice as high for Hispanic males than for white males. There are similar racial divisions among women. Combined state and federal incarceration rates are twice as high for black women as for white women. (Hispanic women are jailed at only a slightly higher rate than white women.) Black and Hispanic inmates make up just over half of all state and federal prisoners.

The Bureau of Justice Statistics Bulletin, "Correctional Populations in the United States, 2013" reports that, at year-end, the United States had a total incarcerated population of 2,3 million people. These inmates were held in the following types of facilities:

- 1,351,000 in state prisons
- 211,000 in federal prisons
- 14,000 in territorial prisons
- 646,000 in local jails
- 33,000 in facilities operated by the Bureau of Immigration and Customs Enforcement
- 1,400 in military facilities
- 2,400 in jails on American Indian lands
- 34,000 held in juvenile or youth facilities

San Quentin State Prison.

Prison and Race

Currently, around 16.6 percent of all adult black males, 7.7 percent of all adult Hispanic males, and 2.6 percent of all adult white males have served time in a state or federal prison. If first-time incarceration rates remain unchanged, the outlook for future generations is quite bleak. About 1 in 4 black males, 1 in 6 Hispanic males, and 1 in 17 white males will be incarcerated in a state or federal prison at some point in their lifetime. For this same generation, approximately 1 in 18 black females, 1 in 50 Hispanic females, and 1 in 50 white females will be incarcerated in a state or federal prison at some point in their life.

Not only are the majority of U.S. prisoners men of minority racial and ethnic groups, they are also generally young. Approximately 55 percent are under the age of 40.

The percentage of black males in prison is much higher than that of white males in prison.

To conclude that race and ethnicity are the direct causes of crime and subsequent imprisonment, however, would be to misinterpret these statistics. The real causes and predictors of crime cannot be seen in the color of a person's skin or inferred from the origin of a person's last name. Currently, the best predictors of crime are poverty and education levels. Statistically, the greater a person's impoverishment and lack of education, the more likely that person is to turn to a life of crime. According to the Bureau of Justice Statistics, only 60 percent of state inmates have their high school diploma or its equivalent. In the United States, black and Hispanic communities, for many complicated historical, social, and political reasons, continue to face the greatest poverty and have the least access to quality education, which leads to higher crime rates in these communities.

The Wheres and Whys

According to the most recent statistics, most state prison inmates are serving time for violent crimes (53 percent), drug crimes (16 percent), or property crimes (19 percent). An additional 11 percent of inmates are imprisoned for **public-order crimes**.

At year-end 2013 the following states had the five highest incarceration rates (per 100,000 members of the population):

Louisiana	1,082
Oklahoma	983
Mississippi	962
Alabama	951
Georgia	916

These states had the five lowest incarceration rates (per 100,000 members of the population):

Maine	285
Minnesota	289
Massachusetts	318
Rhode Island	322
Vermont	335

The type and severity of crime a person commits will determine the type of facility where he or she is incarcerated. The United States has numerous types of incarceration facilities and a number of security levels. The Federal Bureau of Prisons operates facilities of five security levels: minimum, low, medium, high, and administrative.

The Differences between Facility Types

Minimum-security institutions have dormitory-style housing, low staff-to-inmate ratios, limited or no perimeter fencing, and a focus on work and self-improvement programs. Low-security facilities are similar but have a higher staff-to-inmate ratio and double-fenced perimeters. Medium-security facilities have mostly cell-type housing, double-fenced perimeters with electronic surveillance systems or other reinforcement, and higher staff-to-inmate ratios. Work and treatment programs are still widely available. High-security institutions have perimeters with multiple levels of security, such as walls, reinforced fences, watchtowers, and patrols. Inmates are housed in single or multiple-occupant cells, and their movement is

High-security-level prisons, like this California facility, have watchtowers and layers of barbed wire to keep prisoners in.

strictly monitored with a high staff-to-inmate ratio. Administrative facilities are designed to fill special needs in the incarceration system, such as holding offenders who have not yet gone to trial, treating inmates with serious medical conditions, or securing escape-prone inmates. These facilities are designed to accommodate inmates from all security levels.

The security level at which a person is imprisoned greatly influences the type of life that prisoner will lead while behind bars. The security level also affects the monetary costs associated with that person's imprisonment.

Text-Dependent Questions

1. About how many people in the United States are incarcerated? (As in 1 out of how many people are behind bars?)
2. What are the two most common crimes for which state prison inmates have been convicted?
3. Describe the differences between a minimum-security prison and a high-security facility.

Research Projects

1. How is daily life different in a state facility versus a federal facility?
2. Research life behind bars in a military prison facility. What are some benefits afforded inmates? How is it different than a regular prison?

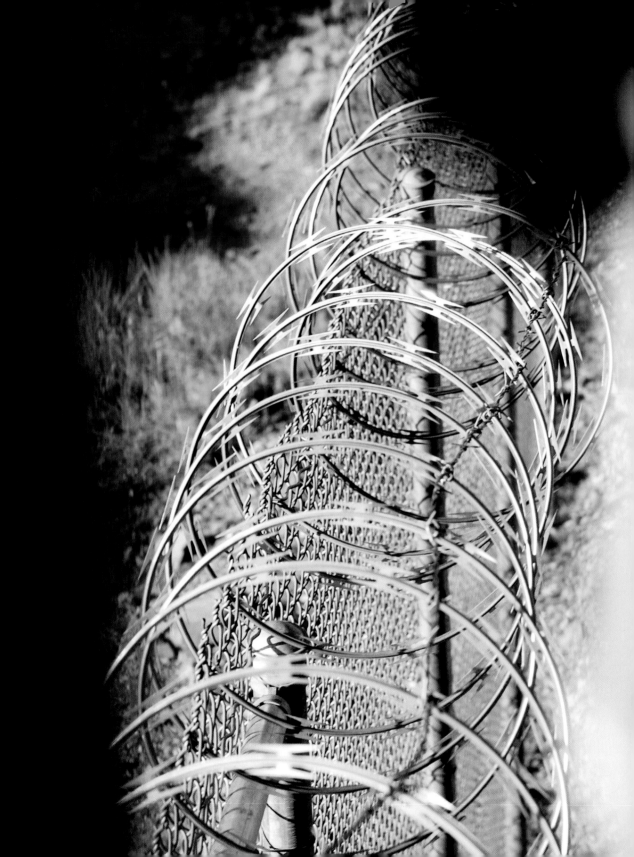

3 The Monetary Costs

Paying the Price of Punishment

According to a special report from the Brookings Institution, the U.S. spends approximately $74 billion on incarceration in one year. The majority of that money is spent on the day-to-day operation of the state incarceration facilities. The other $1.1 billion is spent on capital costs like land, new buildings, or renovations. If divided by all the inmates, the average operating costs for prisons is $32,175 per inmate per year. Both figures average out to approximately $88 per inmate per day. These numbers are, of course, averages. Generally speaking, the lower the security level of a facility, the less that facility costs per inmate to run. The higher the security level, the greater the operational costs.

In the United States approximately 75 percent of state corrections expenditures were on prison operations. Only around 20 percent went to other corrections costs, such as juvenile justice, probation and parole, community-based corrections, and central office administration. The running of prisons requires huge numbers of staff—from administrators, to corrections officers, to nurses in prison medical facilities—and about two-thirds of the money spent on prisons goes to pay for these staff members' salaries, wages, and benefits. The other third pays for operational costs like inmate health care, food, utilities, and supplies. Of the money spent on inmates' basic living needs, the largest portion goes to medical care.

The cost of building and operating prisons costs taxpayers approximately $74 billion each year.

```
                         COPY
              MAIN LINE MENU 9/2 to 9/8, 1946

  1945    BREAKFAST            DINNER                    SUPPER
  M L     Stewed Prunes        Split Pea Soup            Split Pea Soup
  O aD    Bran Flakes          Roast Shoulder of Pork    Boston Baked Beans
  N ba    Fresh Milk           Sage Dressing             Tomato Catsup
    oy    Sugar                Brown Gravy               Beet & Onion Salad
     r    Orange Roll          Mashed Potatoes           Canned Pears
  9-2     Bread & Coffee       Stewed Corn               Bread & Coffee
                               Apple pie
                               Bread & Coffee w/Milk

  T       Apple Sauce          Puree Mongole             Puree Mongole
  U       Cracked Wheat        Baked Meat Loaf           Chili-Con Carne
  E       Fresh Milk           Pan Gravy                 Steamed Rice
  S       Sugar                Steamed Potatoes          Lettuce Salad
          Peanut Roll          Spinach w/Bacon           Crackers
  9-3     Bread & Coffee       Bread & Tea               Layer Cake
                                                         Bread & Coffee

  W       Fresh Orange         Mexican Soup              Mexican Soup
  E       Shredded Wheat       Beef Pot Pie Anglaise     Baked Meat Croquettes
  D       Fresh Milk           Tomato Catsup             Bechamel Sauce
          Sugar                Buttered Beets            Mustard Greens
  9-4     Mapeline Roll        Cole Slaw                 Watermelon
          Bread & Coffee       Bread & Tea               Bread & Coffee

  T       Stewed Peaches       Vegetable Soup            Vegetable Soup
  H       Hot Griddle Cakes    Boiled Corned Beef        Spaghetti & Meat Sauce
  U       Honey                Steamed Potatoes          Romaine Salad
  R       Oleo                 Quick Cooked Cabbage      Spiced Crab Apples
  S       Bread                Prepared Mustard          Bread & Fruit Pudding
          Coffee w/Milk        Bread & Tea               Bread & Coffee
  9-5

  F       Canned Pears         Potato Chowder            Potato Chowder
  R       Farina               Breaded Rock Cod          Two Fried Eggs
  I       Fresh Milk           Sliced Lemon              Fried Potatoes
          Sugar                Mashed Potatoes           Zucchini Saute
          Fruit Roll           Stewed Tomatoes           Iced Cup Cakes
  9-6     Bread & Coffee       Bread & Tea               Bread & Coffee w/Milk.

  S       Canned Plums         Minestrone Soup           Minestrone Soup
  A       Rice Krispies        Stuffed Cabbage, w/Meat   Bacon Jumbolaya
  T       Fresh Milk           Tomatoe Sauce             Tomato Saute
          Sugar                Steamed Potatoes          Cucumber & Onion Salad
  9-7     Mint Roll            Fresh Green Beans         Orange Jello
          Bread & Coffee       Bread & Tea               Bread & Coffee

  S       Half Cantaloupe      Rice Tomato Soup          Rice Tomato Soup
  U       Rolled Oats          Pounded Beef Steak        2 Slices Luncheon Meat
  N       Fresh Milk           Pan Gravy                 Tossed Vegetable Salad
          Sugar                Mashed Potatoes           Apricot Pie
  9-8     Raspberry Bun        Corn on the Cob           Bread & Coffee
          Bread & Coffee       Bread & Coffee

  U.S.P., ALCATRAZ, CALIF.
```

The food served in prisons is not anything to brag about. This 1946 menu from Alcatraz displays the food provided to inmates every day for the week. There are not many choices and no substitutions. The situation has improved but not a lot.

Treating Infectious Diseases

Medical care is an extremely significant monetary cost associated with the incarceration system. States spend approximately $6 billion on medical care for inmates each year. Treatment of infectious diseases makes up a significant portion of those medical costs.

Prisons are ideal **incubators** for disease: they house many people in small, confined spaces, and any time you have many people housed in a very small space, the chances of spreading diseases rise. In some prisons, especially older facilities, poor ventilation systems, dank cells, cockroach infestations, and other unhygienic conditions increase disease transmission. Risky behaviors involving drug use, tattooing, and unsafe sexual practices also contribute to disease transmission. According to the HIV Education Prison Project (HEPP), the most common infectious diseases spread in prison are hepatitis B and hepatitis C. Sexually transmitted diseases, such as syphilis, chlamydia, gonorrhea, and HIV, and respiratory illnesses, such as tuberculosis (TB), are also extremely common.

The $6 billion it costs to provide medical treatment to prisoners each year isn't the only monetary cost racked up as a result of inmates' health. Those who work within prisons are also at great risk of catching illnesses from the prison population, illnesses they will carry home to their families. Similarly, when prisoners are released, those who have contracted illnesses while incarcerated will expose numerous others to disease. Though much more difficult to identify and measure, society incurs additional medical costs whenever those who work in prisons or are released from their prison terms carry infectious diseases to their homes and communities, passing diseases to family members or others they come in close contact with.

The Cost of a Nation of Incarceration

A documentary that looks at the effects of our huge number of inmates.

The Public Health Threat: A Case Study

If one divides prison expenditures by the general population, each person spends an average of $260 on prisons each year. That makes state prison expenditures third in line behind education and health.

A case in Kansas shows how one individual's illness can spread in prison and out, creating a major public health concern. George (not his real name), who was living in a homeless shelter in California, had a suspicious cough and other symptoms that made a doctor at the shelter suspect TB. The doctor recommended a chest X-ray, but George refused to have one. Several months later, he returned to his home in Kansas.

In Kansas, a warrant was out for George's arrest, and he soon turned himself in to the authorities. George spent three days in one jail and seven weeks in a second facility before being released. While in jail, he was diagnosed with bronchial asthma but was never tested for TB. Eight months later, George was convicted and back in jail. Once again, he spent three days in the original jail, and then he was transferred to a third facility where he spent six weeks awaiting sentencing.

By the time George was transferred to a Kansas state prison, he had been jailed for a total of 14 weeks and held in three different facilities. Upon entering the state prison, he underwent routine questioning regarding TB symptoms. George answered six of the seven TB-symptom questions affirmatively, but he was never referred to a doctor for evaluation or diagnosis. George was placed in the general inmate population, and it wasn't until four weeks later that he received a chest X-ray.

George's chest X-ray showed a **lesion** symptomatic of TB, and yet he still spent two more weeks housed among the general inmate population while further tests were conducted. It was only after those tests confirmed TB that George was placed in airborne isolation to protect prison workers and other inmates from this highly infectious disease.

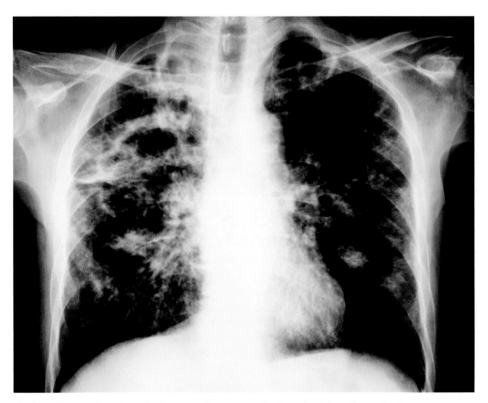

A chest X-ray showing the lungs of a person infected with tuberculosis.

Once health workers determined that George did in fact have TB, an investigation ensued. It attempted to identify all those people George had exposed to infection in the nearly one-year period that had passed since his time in the California homeless shelter. Eventually, the investigation estimated that George had come in contact with approximately 800 people (inmates, prison employees, and others), 318 of whom were identified. Of these, 256 consented to screening and were tested for TB. Forty-seven were diagnosed with latent TB infection (of these, 41 had no previous positive test results for TB). Two, both of whom had been cell mates with George, were diagnosed with TB disease. Although it cannot be proven that any of those diagnosed with TB infection or disease contracted it from George, the likelihood is high that George was in fact the source of exposure for a significant number of those infected. Perhaps more troubling are the nearly 500 people with whom George came in contact who were never identified and could possibly be infected with TB. And the public health danger did not end with George. Each one of those people with whom he had contact in turn had contact with hundreds of others, creating a web of possible infection routes that can never be completely traced.

When a situation like this occurs, numerous health costs will be incurred, not just by the inmates, but also by prison employees, inmate families, and others who are exposed to disease. These medical costs, though directly related to prisons, can be more difficult to identify, track, and link to their source.

A corrections officer on duty in a holding cell area.

Prevention of Illness Is Key

In the United States, many inmates come from impoverished backgrounds; neither they nor their families can afford medical insurance. For those who qualify for government-funded health programs, the costs of their medical care are also ultimately paid for through taxes. However, many people in difficult economic circumstances simply have no health insurance at all. In such circumstances, the individual must pay the medical costs of treating people who contract illnesses from inmates or former inmates. For people who do not have health insurance, however, medical costs may be too great a burden to bear, and of those who are even aware they have contracted an illness, some will choose to forgo medical treatment. Forgoing medical treatment can lead to altogether different costs—such as loss of income for missed time at work, decreased productivity in the workplace, absenteeism from school, and more—that are even more difficult to track and quantify.

How Prisoners Get Tattoos

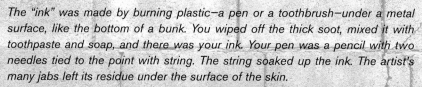

In his book, *Newjack: Guarding Sing Sing*, author and corrections officer, Ted Conover, describes how one inmate received his prison tattoos:

> The "ink" was made by burning plastic—a pen or a toothbrush—under a metal surface, like the bottom of a bunk. You wiped off the thick soot, mixed it with toothpaste and soap, and there was your ink. Your pen was a pencil with two needles tied to the point with string. The string soaked up the ink. The artist's many jabs left its residue under the surface of the skin.

Tattoos are commonplace within the prison system.

The best way to reduce medical costs from diseases contracted in prison is to prevent their spread. To help reduce the transmission of TB in prisons the Advisory Council for the Elimination of Tuberculosis recommends that all prisons, jails, and other correctional institutions develop plans for screening inmates and for dealing with TB infection. So far, only a small percentage of incarceration facilities have such plans in place.

The Canadian Corrections Safe Tattoo Parlor Program

Nearly half of all Canadian inmates get tattoos from other inmates while in prison—and a quarter of inmates have hepatitis C, a disease spread in part by dirty needles used in tattooing. To help control the costs of treating hepatitis C (which can run as much as $20,000 a year per patient) the Corrections Service of Canada launched a program in 2005 that set up tattoo parlors in six Canadian prisons. Inmates were trained in the use of the tattoo equipment, and gave tattoos at a cost of five dollars each. The program was met with applause from many health and **advocacy** organizations in Canada and the United States (including hepatitis expert David Thomas of Johns Hopkins University), but also controversy, as some people don't think taxpayers should have to subsidize prison tattoos. Public outcry led to the program being shut down after just a year.

Overcrowding Spreads Diseases

While risky behaviors, like unsafe tattooing practices, certainly aid in the transmission of bloodborne disease, another significant factor exacerbating the problem of disease transmission within prisons is overcrowding. Overall, the U.S. prison system is operating at 110 percent of its total capacity. Not only are all U.S. prisons full, they are actually holding more people than their cell capacity allows. In many facilities, double-bunking—housing two prisoners in a cell or space designed for one prisoner—is common.

Generally speaking, the housing situation is much worse for federal prisons (which, according to the Bureau of Justice Statistics Bulletin, "Prisons in 2004," are operating at 39 percent above capacity) than for state prisons (17 states' facilities are at least 10 percent above capacity). There are, however, some notable exceptions to this rule. The most severe overcrowding in the country is taking place in California, where things got so bad that in 2009 a federal judge ordered the state to reduce its prison population.

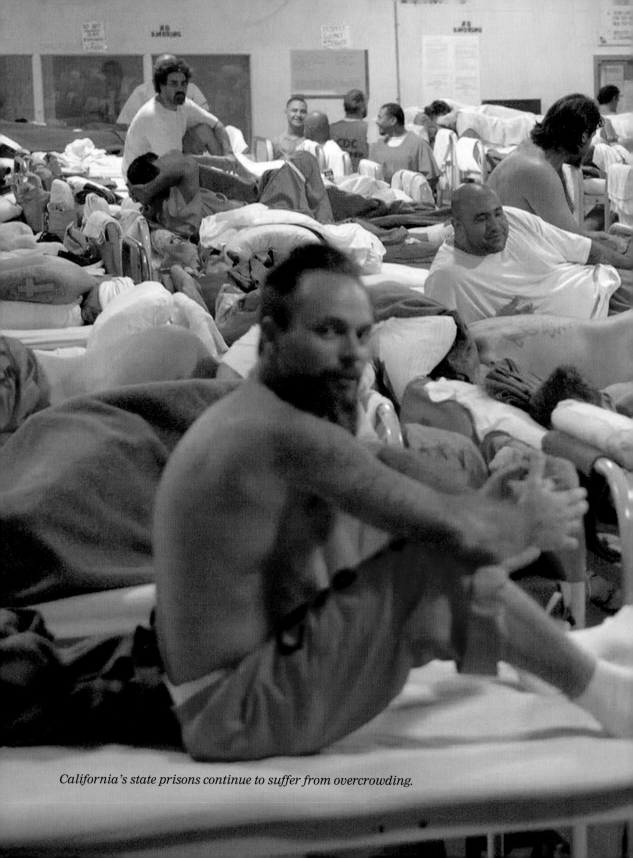

California's state prisons continue to suffer from overcrowding.

A For-Profit Industry

Overcrowding in prisons is a serious problem. Not only does it increase the likelihood of disease transmission, it makes corrections officers' jobs much more difficult. In many cases, overcrowding eliminates the possibility of effectively administering rehabilitative programming and greatly increases the stress and danger corrections officers face. Despite the numerous costs, from facility maintenance to employee wages to inmate medical costs, it would be misleading to imply that prisons simply suck billions of dollars from local, state, and federal budgets. Prisons do, for sure, take a huge amount of money to run, but they can create revenue as well. In fact, in the United States a whole "prison industry" has grown around the incarceration of people. Numerous private companies have decided that, where people are incarcerated, there is money to be made. For example, companies have realized they can decrease labor costs and increase profits by hiring prisoners. Unlike the general population, prisoners have no right to minimum wage, and companies can hire them for just cents a day—or even for no pay at all. But prisons are not simply a good source of cheap labor. The prison itself can be turned into a profitable business.

Convict Leasing in the Post–Civil War South

The post–Civil War period in the American South known as the Reconstruction is among the earliest times that the private sector entered into business with the prison system. As slavery had been abolished, plantation owners needed large numbers of laborers, quickly and cheaply. Many contracted with the federal government to hire prisoners (many of whom were illegally captured and unfairly tried former slaves) to pick cotton and tend to other crops. The practice, known as convict leasing, became incredibly lucrative for both parties—plantation owners had access to a stream of workers, and the government earned a great deal of money. Convict leasing was a major part of the postwar economy in the South. By 1898, about three-quarters of the state of Alabama's income came from convict leasing.

In the United States today, numerous private companies receive contracts from state and federal governments to build and run prisons. The more these companies, some of which are traded on the New York Stock Exchange, can streamline their operations and reduce their costs, the more profit there is to be made from these contracts. *Prison Nation: The Warehousing of America's Poor*, relates the following:

> *A conference sponsored by World Research Group, a New York-based investment firm, informed investors, "While arrests and convictions are steadily on the rise, profits are to be made—profits from crime. Get in on the ground floor of this booming industry now!"*

As of 2016, about 22,000 federal inmates and 91,000 state inmates were held in private facilities around the country. Five states send more than 30 percent of inmates to for-profit facilities: New Mexico (44 percent), Montana (40 percent), Alaska (34 percent), Hawaii (33 percent), and Idaho (30 percent).

Small Town, Big Prisons

It is not just private companies who stand to make money off the incarceration system. Around the United States, many towns (particularly small towns in rural areas that have limited opportunities for economic growth) line up for the chance to have a prison located near them. New prisons need to be built, and that means construction companies will be needed. Existing prisons need to be maintained, which means people and supplies will be required for that maintenance. Prisoners need to be guarded, and that means jobs in corrections. Prisoners need to eat, which means increased revenue for food manufacturers and distributors. Prisoners' families will want to live close to or visit their loved ones; that means a steady flow of incoming people who will pay for apartments, hotels, transportation, food, clothing, and numerous other goods and services. Furthermore, the prisoners themselves will be a source of cheap labor that could potentially attract other businesses or that could be used by the town itself. All these factors make prisons appear to be great economic opportunities for the areas where they will be located.

In 2001, Canada opened its first (and only) privately run adult prison, Central North Correctional Centre located in Penetanguishene, ON. Managed by the American company Management & Training Corporation, the government's contract with the firm was not renewed in 2006. The prison reverted to government control when an analysis found that the privately run facility produced inferior outcomes to similar state-operated prisons.

When a Prison Comes to Town

In the early 1980s, nearly two-thirds of the nation's inmates were held in prisons in metropolitan areas of more than 50,000 people. The economic recession of the 1980s led to a fundamental shift: by the mid-1990s, nearly 70 percent of inmates were serving time in facilities in rural areas with populations of less than 10,000 people. As a way to boost the economy in the late 1980s, 190 state prisons were built, entirely in small towns and rural areas. Many people in those towns thought a prison would lead to more jobs and an economic boom, but an Iowa State University study found that, although towns with newly built prisons may have received some new jobs they had less growth in businesses, wages, and real estate.

Are They Good For Communities?

The potential monetary benefits of prisons can be very seductive to towns desperate for an economic boost, but other costs usually follow when a prison moves into town. Some are unexpected monetary costs, such as a decrease in property values close to the facility, loss of local jobs as companies switch to cheaper prison labor, or an increase in the cost of goods and services that are in high demand by the prison and resulting larger population. However, far more troubling to these communities are the costs that cannot be easily measured and discussed in terms of dollars and cents. There are social costs that result from the way prisons are run, the people associated with them, and the activities that continue to surround the, albeit incarcerated, criminal population. For example, many towns find that when a prison moves in, a burgeoning drug trade follows; gang activity grows; a poor, uneducated, and **transient** population develops; cases of infectious diseases rise; and stress-related illnesses, domestic tensions, and abuse develop in the families of corrections workers. These are just some of the social costs associated with incarceration.

Text-Dependent Questions

1. About what percentage of prison budgets is allocated to day-to-day operations?
2. What's the average daily cost of housing an inmate?
3. What are some of the most commonly spread communicable diseases behind bars?

Research Projects

1. Research some ways that inmates are being educated about TB, HIV/AIDS, and hepatitis behind bars. Have these programs affected infection rates?
2. Similar to the Canadian prisoner tattoo program, research another innovative, if controversial, approach to corrections and/or disease control.

4 The Social Costs

The Effect on Families

Prisons can bring negative social consequences to the towns where they are located, the people who work in them, and the families of prison employees. The greatest social cost of the incarceration system, however, is borne by the families of prisoners (especially their children) and the communities where they lived before entering prison and to which they will return on release.

Those who are imprisoned often leave behind a family that must adjust to life without their loved one. In the United States today, 2.7 million children have an incarcerated parent. The following stories show some of the ways in which families struggle to adjust when one of their members goes to jail or prison. Although these stories are based on true families, in each case names and details have been altered to protect identities.

Finding the Positive

When Frank lost his driver's license, due to driving while intoxicated, and was sentenced to a jail term, his 56-year-old wife, Eunice, found herself in a very difficult position. She had never learned to drive. Frank had always dropped Eunice

The greatest social cost of the incarceration system is borne by the families of prisoners (especially their children) and the communities where they lived before entering prison and to which they will return on release.

off at her job on his way to work and picked her up on his way home. But now Eunice would have to pick her husband up from the jail each morning, drive him to his job (he had qualified for a **work-release program**), and then return him to the jail at the end of the day.

Learning to drive and obtaining her driver's license presented a huge challenge for Eunice. She met that challenge, however, and successfully transported her husband to and from the jail and got herself to and from her own job each day. Living alone was also a challenge; Eunice was often lonely and sometimes frightened, especially at night. But she managed these trials as well. And she was able to see the benefits of her situation. Although her husband was in jail, they were very lucky. At least he was still able to work. Without her husband's income, Eunice never would have been able to make the house payments by herself. When Frank's jail time was over, they still had their home and their jobs. Eventually, Frank was able to get his driver's license back as well, and Frank and Eunice basically returned to the life they'd always had.

Although Eunice certainly would have preferred that her husband had never gone to jail at all, she is able to identify one other positive outcome from the experience. She says that had Frank not gone to jail, she never would have learned to drive. The entire situation, though very trying, forced Eunice to learn to be more independent. Frank died five years ago, and now that Eunice must live on her own once more, she finds herself thankful for the skills she was forced to develop during Frank's jail term.

A Family Destroyed

In contrast to Frank and Eunice's story, Jamal can't find anything positive that resulted from his father's imprisonment. Jamal is the second of four children, and he was just eight years old when his father went to prison for assaulting a police officer.

Jamal recalls that, prior to his father's imprisonment, the family struggled financially but was still able to meet all their basic needs and pay their rent. Once his father went to prison, however, life changed dramatically. Jamal's mother couldn't make ends meet on her minimum-wage job. With four children to support, car payments to make, and bills and rent to pay, there was rarely enough money each month. Often Jamal's mother would sit down and debate which bill to pay: the rent or the car. More often than not, she reasoned that the car was an absolute necessity because there was no public transportation where they lived. Without the car she couldn't get to her job.

The situation led to a string of evictions. Jamal recalls that the family was rarely able to make more than two or three months' rent. Some landlords would cut the family a bit of slack, at first allowing the mother of four to make a late payment or two, even sometimes allowing a few months to go by with no payment at all. But eventually, they all had to make the same decision; if they didn't kick the family out, they would make no money from their rental property. And so Jamal's family would move, always to a new neighborhood where their reputation had not preceded them.

But it wasn't changing houses that affected Jamal and his siblings the most; it was switching schools, five times between his father's imprisonment and his freshman year of high school. Jamal's grades suffered, but he felt the social repercussions were just as devastating. He was perpetually a new kid in a new school. He never had friends, and he never had a significant relationship with a teacher. The situation was even worse for Jamal's younger brother. He had a serious learning disability, but with moving from school to school, his learning disability wasn't identified until junior high. By that time, he was already far behind his peers in every subject.

Despite the family's struggles, by his sophomore year of high school, Jamal felt like things were beginning to improve. His father had been released from prison, but his mother no longer wanted anything to do with him, and the children didn't know where he was. However, Jamal's mom had a better job now, and, although they didn't always make all their bills, they had managed to live in the same house and attend the same school for two years. For the first time, Jamal had friends, was involved in school activities, and had some teachers who had taken an interest in his situation and were encouraging him to go to college. He was on the football team and was a star of the wrestling team. He also loved music and was very active in the school band.

Then tragedy struck. Jamal's mother was killed when a drunk driver struck her vehicle. Their mother had long been estranged from her own family, and with their father's whereabouts unknown and their mother gone, the four children found themselves isolated and alone. Jamal's older brother was 17, and he tried to hold the family together. He had no job, however, and they now had no car. Then Jamal's father showed up and said he was there to take care of the family. The children were relieved to have their father home.

Jamal doesn't know if his father's character was just flawed from childhood or if prison changed him. Jamal does, however, believe that had his father never gone to prison, had he instead spent those years developing a relationship with his children, he wouldn't have done what he did next.

When the insurance settlement money from his mother's accident arrived, Jamal's father took it, told the children he was going to find them a better house, and disappeared. A month went by, and they did not see or hear from him. Then one day, he showed up again. This time he took the children's Social Security checks (being under eighteen, they couldn't cash them without their father's signature) and again took off. For a year, this was the family's pattern, Jamal's father disappearing for weeks and even months at a time and rarely leaving the children with enough money to pay for food. If it wasn't for a few concerned friends and neighbors who offered rides when the children needed to go somewhere and who occasionally bought them some groceries, Jamal's not sure how they would have made it through the year.

Jamal's father always insisted he was looking for a house, but the house never materialized. At the end of the school year, the children moved with their father to the city, where he led them to believe he had an apartment waiting. This, however,

was untrue, and the children found themselves sleeping on a string of apartment floors belonging to their father's friends and associates. Eventually, the family broke up. Offered a place at a friend's house, Jamal moved back to the earlier town and returned to his school; he was able to go to college on a scholarship. After two years, Jamal's younger brother also moved in with a friend in the same town and returned to high school. Their younger sister now lives with a family friend in the city. She's an A student, but she bears emotional scars from her ordeal and is encountering social and behavioral difficulties. Their older brother has worked a string of dead-end jobs, and Jamal suspects he is now involved in criminal activity. Jamal's father is back in prison, this time serving a sentence for armed robbery.

Fifty-two percent of state inmates and 63 percent of federal inmates have at least one child under the age of 18. Ninety-two percent of incarcerated parents are male. Forty-seven percent of fathers and 57 percent of mothers in prison are serving time for violent offenses. Sixty-two percent of mothers and 59 percent of fathers are serving time for drug offenses.

Families: The Unheard Victims of Prison Sentences

The anguish suffered by the innocent families of prisoners.

Lives on Hold

Catalina and Robert did not have a close relationship when Robert went to prison. Robert was 18 and in his senior year of high school. He had already been in trouble on a number of occasions and had spent time in a juvenile detention center, but now he was in much bigger trouble. He had been stealing prescription drugs from another kid at school and selling them. Suddenly, Robert was going to prison for drug trafficking.

Catalina was 20 and hadn't finished high school. Just three months earlier, her one-year-old son, Samuel, had required medical attention. An unexpected result of the blood work was that it showed Robert to be Samuel's father, rather than the man with whom she was living. When Catalina's boyfriend kicked her and Samuel out, they went to live with Robert at his mother's house.

The situation was tense. Catalina and Robert had a son, but no relationship. They didn't love or trust each other, they were both seeing other people, and they didn't know how they were supposed to interact. Robert had no idea how to begin being a father. To make matters worse, Samuel didn't recognize Robert as his father and wanted nothing to do with him. Furthermore, Catalina found herself resenting Robert and his mother suddenly offering opinions and making parenting decisions regarding her son. The situation was truly a mess when Robert was imprisoned.

In some cases, juvenile offenders are treated similarly to adults.

Catalina and Robert were going through a difficult period of adjustment when Robert left for prison, and now Catalina feels like their lives are on hold. She often feels like an unwelcome stranger living in Robert's mother's house, a situation that was made worse when Catalina's second child, this one not Robert's, was born. She has had trouble finding and keeping a job. Currently, Robert's mother is supporting herself, her youngest child, Catalina, and Catalina's two children on her minimum-wage job and the child-support payments she receives from her ex-husband. Catalina considers moving out with her children and going on welfare, but she's afraid of being on her own and isn't sure she wants to separate Samuel from Robert's family.

Catalina thinks that, had Robert not gone to prison, maybe the situation would be better. He could be working to help support the family, and he could be forming a relationship with Samuel. As things stand, Samuel will be at least three years old before Robert is released. Catalina thinks that Samuel might never accept Robert as his father, and she worries even more about the type of father Robert might turn out to be. Catalina will be the first to admit that she doesn't really know Robert that well and that, so far, Robert has not been the best role model for their son. But she has little belief that prison will rehabilitate Robert and make him a better man and parent. In fact, her greatest fear is that Robert will emerge from prison even worse than when he went in.

Children, Families, and Former Prisoners All Suffer

[A]n increasing number of prisoners are returning home, having spent longer terms behind bars, less prepared for life on the outside, with less assistance in their reintegration and, at best, strained connections to their families and communities. Often they will have difficulties reconnecting with jobs, housing, and perhaps their families when they return, and many remain plagued by substance abuse and health problems. Most will be rearrested and many will be returned to prison for new crimes or parole violations. And this cycle of removal and return of large numbers of individuals, mostly men (although the number of incarcerated women is growing exponentially), is increasingly concentrated in a relatively small number of communities that already encounter enormous social and economic disadvantages. The families in these neighborhoods are those most impacted.

In short, the children, families, and former prisoners impacted by incarceration may represent a group more at risk than any other subculture in the country.

(From the U.S. Department of Health and Human Services' "Background Paper: The Effect of Incarceration and Reentry on Children, Families, and Communities")

When in prison, you cannot pick or choose the times that you would like to spend with your family. Visiting hours are set by the prison, and prisoners are usually separated from their family by a piece of glass.

Struggling to Rebuild Lives

As the preceding examples show, the social costs to families of prisoners are many. They range from comparatively minor challenges—like Eunice needing to learn to drive and be independent—to major economic struggles—like those Jamal's family faced. Families of inmates worry, as Catalina does, about how their loved ones will change and whether they will bring the unhealthy attitudes and violence they encounter in prison back home when they are released. Like Jamal, his siblings, and Samuel, children of prisoners lose the opportunity to bond with their parents and often live without the structure, discipline, and role models necessary for healthy development.

But the social costs of incarceration to the families of prisoners aren't just those they face while their loved one is incarcerated. Additional costs will affect the families once their loved ones return home.

Even when a person's prison term is over, the effects of incarceration carry on. The majority of prisoners are young men in the prime of their life. Their peers outside the prison walls are spending these years earning educations, gaining work experience, and building careers. When prisoners are released after years in prison, they are unable to compete for good jobs. While in prison, most receive little training that will help them once outside, so even on release, the individual may be no more able to support himself or his family than when he was behind bars. It is estimated that approximately 25 percent of inmates participate in no vocational or educational programs at all.

Many individuals also leave prison socially and emotionally ill equipped to make decisions for themselves. In prison, a prisoner is told what to do at every moment of the day: when to wake, when to eat, when to shower, when to work, when to sleep. After a long stint behind bars, many individuals find themselves no longer able to make the simple day-to-day decisions necessary to function successfully in the larger society. To make matters even worse, many will struggle with an addiction or illness that wasn't properly treated while they were there.

Many people would argue that the social costs to families and communities are unfortunate but justifiable by-products of what is otherwise a worthwhile and necessary system. The greatest social benefit of prisons is undoubtedly the fact that they **quarantine** from the general population thousands of dangerous criminals who would otherwise be free to harm other people. But does this benefit mean that the more people we incarcerate, the safer society will be? Many experts say no.

Mentor programs are one way of keeping ex-convicts from returning to prison. Ex-con Tim (right) shares an incredible relationship with his mentor Phil. Tim says having a mentor, after serving two stints in prison, helped him in a major way, to assimilate back into the world after his release.

Crime Rates Are Falling but the Prison Population Keeps Growing

While incarceration rates have been steadily climbing for decades and are expected to continue doing so into the foreseeable future, crime rates have actually been in decline or stagnating for approximately a decade. Proponents of "tough on crime" sentencing laws and the current incarceration system would like to argue that the drop in crime (which has been particularly in the areas of violent crime and property offenses) is in fact due to the higher incarceration rates: more criminals behind bars equals fewer crimes carried out on the streets. However, there is no evidence linking higher incarceration rates to lower crime rates. In fact, in state-by-state comparisons, those with high incarceration rates often continue to have higher crime rates than states with low incarceration rates.

One of the possible reasons for ever-increasing incarceration rates despite decreasing crime rates is stiff sentencing practices. Mandatory sentences and longer terms, specifically for drug-related offenses, have swelled the prison ranks. The Obama administration made great strides to reduce the population of federal prisoners, specifically those held on drug charges. During his presidency, President Obama ordered the release of or shortened the sentences of nearly 700 inmates serving long spells for minor drug offenses, commending those who completed diversion or rehabilitation programs. "Let's reward prisoners with reduced sentences if they complete programs that make them less likely to repeat an offense," Obama said in 2015.

It may be difficult to imagine how more people can be going to prison when fewer people are committing crimes, but the following hypothetical example explains how such a thing can happen. Imagine in one city 15 years ago, 50 people were convicted of crimes, but only 30 were sentenced to prison terms. The rest received community service, probation, or other lesser punishments. In the same city 15 years later, however, only 40 people are convicted of crimes. However, with the tougher sentencing laws, 35 of the 40 receive prison terms, while only 5 receive lesser punishments. The city 15 years later has a lower crime rate but a higher incarceration rate.

Imprisoning more and more people for nonviolent crimes may come at a great social cost beyond that exacted upon the families of those inmates. Although a goal of the incarceration system is meant to be reform, studies show us that the current prison system in the United States is doing virtually nothing to rehabilitate criminals. Inmates often leave prison even less prepared (or at least no more prepared) to hold a job and to function successfully in society than when they first entered prison. Not only does prison not prepare inmates for life on the outside, it often exacts mental, emotional, and physical tolls that reduce individuals' ability to succeed outside prison walls. Recidivism rates—the rates at which former inmates return to prison—are alarmingly high. And sometimes excons return to the streets as even more hardened criminals than when they left. In many ways, prisons can serve as "schools of crime," lesser criminals learning worse criminal activity from fellow inmates, or nonviolent offenders becoming violent in the high-stress, dangerous environment of prison.

Illegal drugs, such as opium, are commonly seized by police in the war on drugs.

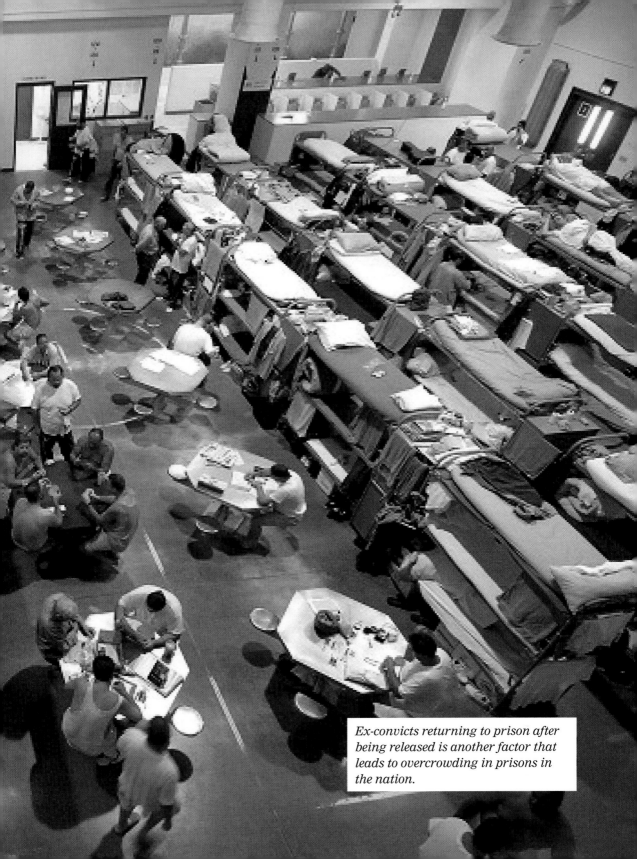

Ex-convicts returning to prison after being released is another factor that leads to overcrowding in prisons in the nation.

Vocational training programs

Many prisons offer vocational training, which teaches inmates a skill that they can use during their prison work duty as well as in the outside world upon their release. Among the most common vocational training programs offered are plumbing, electrical work, carpentry, sewing, landscaping, and food service. One federal facility in Virginia even teaches inmates computer-aided design.

Prisoners working in a sewing workshop.

Prison Workers Pay a Price Too

Families of prisoners and the communities from which prisoners come and to which they return on release are not the only groups paying the social costs of incarceration. Prisons exact huge tolls on the people who work within their walls as well. For his book, *Newjack: Guarding Sing Sing*, **anthropologist** and author Ted Conover applied to become a New York State corrections officer in order to get inside prison walls and experience prison life firsthand. He was accepted and spent the next year training for the position and then working in New York's Sing Sing prison. In the book, Conover recalls a union representative describing the job as, "a life sentence in eight-hour shifts." In Conover's experience, this statement is all too true. For a corrections officer, every moment spent working within prison walls is a moment spent in an incarceration of its own kind. While at work, corrections officers are vulnerable to the dangerous community they are guarding. They are verbally and mentally abused by the inmates. They can contract illnesses that circulate throughout the prison. They can be injured, taken hostage, or even killed. They often fear that they or their family will be targeted for violence when certain inmates are released. They also know that when inmates are released, they themselves could encounter the inmates at the grocery store, the gas station, and other venues of daily life. A prisoner may also be a powerful or prominent figure in the correction officer's community, which could have implications as well.

The high-stress work environment of prisons takes a huge mental, emotional, and physical toll on corrections workers. As reported in Joycelyn M. Pollock's *Prisons and Prison Life: Costs and Consequences*, corrections officers suffer from higher rates of alcoholism, heart disease, divorce, **hypertension**, emotional disorders, and other stress-related conditions than the general population.

Corrections officers stand at the receiving window where inmates are checked into the prison system.

Bringing Home the Stress

Although corrections officers generally strive to leave work at the prison gate, all too often the stress and negative consequences they experience at work find their way into officers' homes and affect their spouses, children, and other family members. Ted Conover recalls experiencing exactly this phenomenon. He describes coming home at the end of a hard day at the prison and caring for his two young children for a few hours before his wife returned from her own job:

> *Between the time I . . . let the babysitter go and the time my wife came home, I had about two hours. Two hours, it sometimes seemed, to get healthy, because the kids were pure and I was dirty. My daughter, one, and son, now three, would be thrilled to see me, and I treasured this time together. But it could also be the worst time of the day, because in a way, I'd been dealing with difficult children all day long.*

Conover goes on to describe an incident one day when, after a particularly bad shift at the prison, his nerves were completely frayed. His son was having a challenging, rambunctious day, and his wife had to work late. Conover relates that when his son went running upstairs to wake his sleeping sister, something within Conover "sort of snapped." He surprised himself by spanking his son and felt horrible afterward, knowing that striking out in this way had much more to do with being unable to cope with the stress in his life than with his son's difficult behavior. Reflecting on these difficult weeks, Conover remarks, "I'd never been meaner or more vulnerable."

For Conover, working as a corrections officer ended when one year was up. While working in the prison, he was often able to console himself by remembering the fact that he had only a few more months to go—that this wasn't his life, it was an

Reentry in Action

The state of Virginia's Department of Corrections offers a three-step gradual-release program that begins to prepare offenders for release two months ahead of time. The first phase: programming, in which inmates attend six to eight weeks of a series of classes, including Life Skills, Conflict Resolution, and Anger Management. The second phase: work release, in which inmates are let out of prison for a few hours each day under the direction of a local business. After the successful completion of those two phases comes the third phase, or community release. Similar to parole or probation, the now former inmates are on their own to integrate back into the community, but with ongoing access to character-building resources and social services.

experiment. At times, he was able to separate himself and his emotions by taking notes, being an observer, playing the part of the anthropologist. Most corrections officers, however, can't separate themselves this way and won't be leaving their job within a year's time. For many of them, the stress they bring home to their spouses and children manifests itself in much more than a yell or a spank.

Anger and Open Hatred on the Job

I gave up trying to figure out if the inmates arrived on the row behaving like animals or if the unit made them that way. Just working in the place was degrading. The environment was charged with anger and open hatred between convicts and guards. Inmates routinely threw feces and urine at us, hooded their cells, and stopped up toilets. Officers and trusty workers—patience depleted and nerves frayed—responded with brute force.

—A FORMER CORRECTIONS OFFICER QUOTED IN *PRISONS AND PRISON LIFE: COSTS AND CONSEQUENCES* BY JOYCELYN M. POLLOCK

Reflecting on the experience of being a corrections officer and how it affected himself, his family, his coworkers, and the prisoners he oversaw, Ted Conover ultimately asks, "What did it do to a man when his work consisted of breaking the spirit of other men? And who invented this lose–lose game anyway?" In asking this question, Conover moves from examining the monetary and social costs of prisons, to asking a fundamental moral question. The incarceration system involves more moral challenges than perhaps any other system in society.

Text-Dependent Questions

1. How many children in the United States have an incarcerated parent?
2. How many inmates serving time have children on the outside?
3. What hardline government initiatives have led to an explosion in the prison population?

Research Projects

1. Research the effects of being a prison guard. Does it have a measurable impact on long-term psychological health?
2. Research crime rates for children of parents who spent a significant amount of time in prison. Are they more or less likely to commit crimes themselves?

 # The Moral Costs

Words to Understand

Indelible: Something that cannot be removed or erased.

Plea bargains: The negotiations of agreements between prosecutors and defendants whereby defendants are permitted to plead guilty to reduced charges.

Viability: A reasonable chance to succeed.

Should Prisons Be Run for Profit?

When people debate the morality of the incarceration system, they are basically questioning whether the system is "right" or "wrong," whether it is "good" or "bad." When it comes to incarceration, there are numerous moral debates to be had.

One of the hottest debates concerning incarceration in the last decade is over private prisons. The United States, which at one point had as many as 140 such facilities, has certainly seen some economic benefits to contracting out the care of prisoners to private companies. For example, a 2015 report by the Bureau of Prisons found that a private prison could house an inmate for $63 per day, versus $80 for a government-run facility. But does economic **viability** mean that private prisons are positive things? Many people don't believe so, and the reason is simple: how can it be morally sound to have companies with a financial interest in people's incarceration? Can such institutions effectively promote rehabilitation and crime reduction when their profits depend on the existence of a prisoner population? They have a conflict of interest: they cannot fulfill the role the incarceration system is meant to play in reducing crime and rehabilitating criminals, because if too many people are rehabilitated and too little crime is committed, they will go out of business. For some people, this is reason enough to declare incarceration systems that contract prison management to private companies morally unsound.

In August 2016, Deputy Attorney General Sally Q. Yates projected that the federal Bureau of Prisons estimated that it would house 14,200 inmates in for-profit

Critics argue that forcing inmates to work without pay is a form of slave labor, and therefore immoral. Here, a work crew of inmates clears weeds from a city park in Phoenix, AZ.

prisons. That's way down from the 30,000 incarcerated in private prisons in 2013. For that reason and more, Yates announced that the federal government would begin to phase out its use of private prisons. That's on the federal level; individual states continue to contract their use.

Is Prison Labor Slave Labor?

A related moral issue is the use of prison labor by local, state, and federal governments, and by private corporations. Many prisoners perform work, such as food service or cleaning, within the prison, and in the United States, this work is unpaid. In addition, prisoners may work within or outside of the prison producing goods and services for governments or private companies. If prisoners are paid at all for this work, it is extremely little, often just cents a day.

Critics argue that such a system is a form of slave labor, and therefore immoral. They believe that incarcerated or not, people should not be compelled to work without pay. The situation is made more morally complex by the fact that so many inmates have families and children who are struggling in poverty in their absence. And poverty is involved in the moral issues surrounding the incarceration system in another way.

The Moral and Ethical Costs of Mass Incarceration

The American criminal justice system is the largest in the world. What is that doing to our democracy?

Prisons, Poverty, and Education

In effect, the prison system has become the preferred method in the United States for dealing with the effects of poverty and lack of education. There is no doubt that a great deal of crime, especially drug-related crime and property offenses, is the result of poverty. But while the state and federal governments have been putting ever-greater funds toward expanding the prison system, they have reduced funds for welfare and other programs that are meant to help address poverty.

In her book *Prisons and Prison Life: Costs and Consequences*, Joycelyn M. Pollock states that, according to one study, "states' welfare spending was negatively associated with the incarceration rate. In other words, states with generous welfare benefits had lower incarceration rates, and states that had very low welfare spending had the highest incarceration rates."

While tough sentencing laws, mandatory sentences for drug offenses, "three strikes and you're out" policies, and an increased reliance on incarceration have never been shown to actually reduce crime, reducing poverty and increasing education have. But today, many states are still more focused on building new prisons than on reaching out to the poor and uneducated. In *Newjack: Guarding Sing Sing*, one inmate, Larson, discusses this mentality—a mentality that focuses more on punishing crime than on trying to prevent it—with Corrections Officer Conover. Conover relates the conversation:

You could feel the rush of prison growth even in the forgotten backwater of Sing Sing, where the superintendent had said that getting money to build new and bigger vocational shops was his number-one priority.

"I'd die to stop that," Larson said, to my surprise.

"You don't want to see this place improve?"

"No. The money should all be put back into the poor neighborhoods, back into education for children, to change the things that send people here. . . . Dig this. Anyone planning a prison they're not going to build for ten or fifteen years is planning for a child, planning prison for somebody who's a child right now. So you see? They've already given up on that child. They already expect that child to fail. You heard? Now why, if you could keep that from happening, if you could send that child to a good school and help his family stay together—if you could do that, why are you spending that money to put him in jail?"

I had no answer for Larson. He had made me feel dumb in my uniform, like a bozo carrying out someone else's ill-conceived plan. But he didn't act as if I were to blame.

This is the heart of the moral argument against America's current incarceration system—that the country has been more focused on getting "tough on crime" and "putting criminals away" than on changing the circumstances that produce criminals in the first place. In doing so, a large portion of America's youth has been abandoned, left to find their own way in the country's most poverty-stricken areas—areas where drugs, gangs, and violence rule and where people turn to crime just to survive.

Mentally Ill Prisoners

Yet another moral debate surrounding America's incarceration system is the rate at which the mentally ill are incarcerated and held with little or no treatment in prisons. The U.S. Department of Health and Human Services "Background Paper: The Effect of Incarceration and Reentry on Children, Families, and Communities" reports that rates of mental illness are between two and four times higher among inmates than the general population. Many of these suffer from conditions like schizophrenia/psychosis, bipolar disorder, and posttraumatic stress disorder— all conditions that affect a person's perception of reality and could be extremely influential in whatever crimes that person commits. However, since many of the mentally ill accused of crimes are also poor, they may not have access to health care professionals and adequate legal counsel—raising the question, were these individuals truly mentally competent when they committed their crimes, or were they found guilty because they lacked the mental capacity, health care professionals, and legal representation to prove their innocence or mental incompetence?

According to a 2010 study by the National Center on Addiction and Substance Abuse, only 11 percent of prisoners with substance abuse problems incarcerated in state-run facilities received professional substance-abuse treatment.

Racism

Many people argue that as long as incarceration is the primary response to the effects of drugs, poverty, and failed educational systems, the U.S. justice and incarceration systems will be racist—another serious moral flaw. Respected academic Noam Chomsky believes this racist tendency is more intentional and overt than most people realize. In his article, "Drug Policy as Social Control," Chomsky argues that the war on drugs, which is responsible for the incarceration of so many of today's prisoners (particularly poor, black prisoners), is in essence a means of controlling America's minority population—a population that, if ever it became politically united, could be dangerous to those who currently hold America's social, economic, and political power (and who happen to be mostly white). Chomsky argues that education, not prison, is the best way to deal with America's drug problem, but he points out the following:

> Today educational programs are on the decline; they're being cut back. The circumstances driving people to use drugs are intensifying. There's more poverty and fewer jobs, lower wages and fewer support systems. That's what's driving people to drugs, and that's where the problem lies. But it's not being approached because the drug problem has been converted into a means of social control.

Access to adequate legal representation is a major factor in the huge numbers of poor and minority inmates behind bars.

Access to Adequate Legal Representation

The war on drugs and higher crime rates are not the only things driving America's poverty-stricken, minority communities behind bars. The fact that people of impoverished backgrounds so often cannot afford adequate legal counsel is another major influence leading to the incarceration of the poor. In his article, "The Accused Get What the System Doesn't Pay For: Poor Legal Representation for People Who Can't Afford Lawyers," Stephen B. Bright states the following:

> *Eighty percent of people accused of crimes are unable to afford a lawyer to defend them. While public defender offices or dedicated lawyers capably defend some of the accused, far more are assigned lawyers who work under crushing caseloads, are paid so little that they devote little time to the cases, and lack the time, knowledge, resources, and often even the inclination to defend a case properly. The result is coerced guilty pleas or unfair trials, unreliable verdicts, and sentences that do not fit the crime or the person convicted.*

Lack of adequate legal counsel for poor people accused of crimes is a pressing practical and moral issue in the U.S. justice system. In the United States, all people accused of a crime are supposed to be "innocent until proven guilty." But many poor people (especially those with little education), under the advisement of inadequate legal counsel or with no legal counsel at all, accept **plea bargains** and prison terms rather than risk going to trial. Sometimes, faced with the prospect of extremely harsh penalties if they lose at trial, people will accept plea bargains and prison terms even when they are not guilty of the crime. When such a thing happens, not only is it a crime against the wrongly accused, it is a crime against society: for every innocent person behind bars, there is a criminal still roaming the streets.

Joe Frank Cannon, a lawyer in Houston, TX, exemplifies the inadequate counsel that is often assigned to poor people who cannot afford lawyers. It was well known among Houston judges that Cannon tended to snooze through his clients' trials. Nevertheless, he was able to represent people for more than 40 years, often appointed to the cases of poor people because he had a reputation for being able to speed through his caseloads, moving his clients quickly in and out of their trials, and therefore keeping the judges' courtrooms moving. Cannon has had 10 clients sentenced to death, more than almost any other lawyer in the entire state. And even though court records show that he was asleep during portions of some of these trials, the convictions have not been overturned. One client that caused Cannon to nod off, Carl Johnson, has been executed.

Cases such as Carl Johnson's raise what is perhaps the greatest moral debate concerning the prison system: the debate over capital punishment—the death penalty. The United States is, in fact, one of the few industrialized nations in the world that still has the death penalty. Not all states subscribe to capital punishment, but 36 of them, plus the federal government, do. Twenty-eight inmates were executed by states in 2015. Texas, by far, was responsible for the most, with 13. The other inmates executed that year were in Florida (2), Georgia (5), Missouri (6), Oklahoma (1), and Virginia (1). In all, the United States had 2,943 prisoners on death row at the end of 2015.

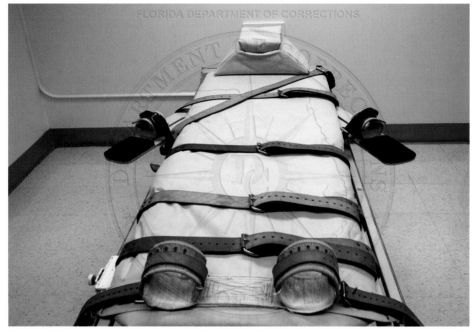

The lethal injection gurney used at Florida State Prison.

One very significant cost of the death penalty is the toll it takes on those who must carry out the sentence. In any case in which a person is put to death, a team of people, including one doctor, must oversee and administer that death. Killing another human being, even one responsible for the most heinous of crimes, always leaves an emotional scar. Even the most professional and experienced doctors and corrections employees are not immune to the **indelible** mark the death sentence leaves behind.

Nor does it seem to be an especially effective crime deterrent. Many larger states, including New York and North Carolina, have abolished the death penalty altogether, or placed a hold on executing prisoners until more research can be conducted. Even without the death penalty in place to scare potential criminals, murder rates in both the states have dropped. This suggests the lack of a connection between the death penalty and crime prevention.

Text-Dependent Questions

1. At its peak, the United States had about how many for-profit prisons?
2. In 2015, what was the cost comparison for housing inmates in a public facility versus a private one?
3. What was the main factor in the federal government's decision to phase out the use of private prisons?
4. What percentage of prisoners with substance abuse problems receive treatment for their issue?

Research Projects

1. How are private prisons able to save money in ways government-run prisons cannot? What are some of their cost-cutting measures?
2. How does daily life differ for inmates at a private prison? Have any former inmates written about their experiences across the two types of facilities?

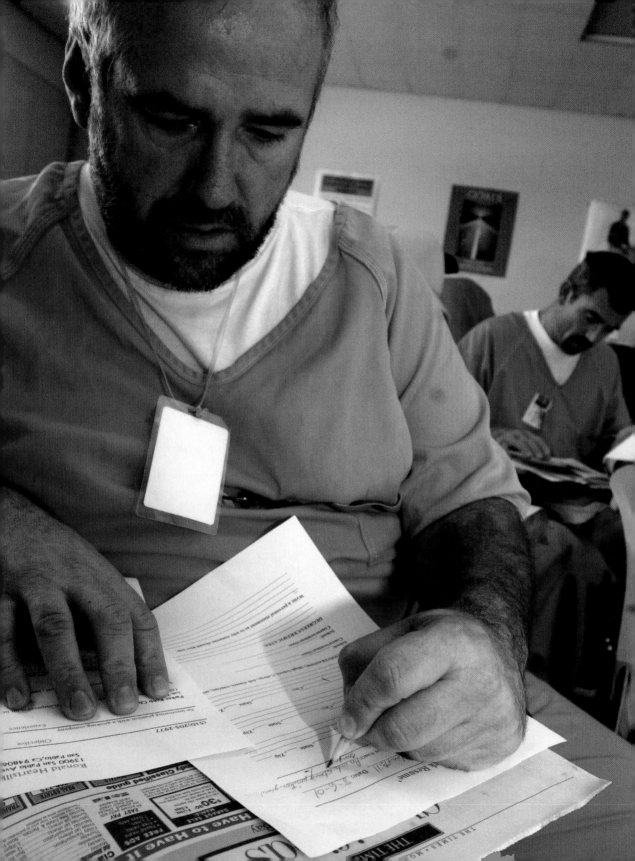

6 Need for Prison Reform?

The Point of Prisons

The top government agency that oversees incarceration and other forms of corrections in the United States is the Federal Bureau of Prisons. Technically a division of the Department of Justice, the Bureau of Prisons operates all prisons on the federal level (and until recently, contracted the use of private facilities) and its more than 1.5 million inmates. (It does not directly control state prisons.)

The vision statement of the Federal Bureau of Prisons is as follows:

> *The Federal Bureau of Prisons, judged by any standard, is widely and consistently regarded as a model of outstanding public administration, and as the best value provided of efficient, safe and humane correctional service and programs in America.*

> *The bureau believes this vision will be realized when the following goals are achieved:*

Education and job opportunity are the best ways to keep people out of prison and from returning once they've been released. Here, soon-to-be-released inmates attend a jobs skills class where they are preparing resumes to apply for jobs.

The bureau provides for public safety by assuring that no escapes or disturbances occur in its facilities.

- *The bureau ensures the physical safety of all inmates through a controlled environment which meets each inmate's need for security through the elimination of violence, predatory behavior, gang activity, drug use, and inmate weapons.*

- *Through the provision of health care, mental, spiritual, educational, vocational, and work programs, inmates are well-prepared for a productive and crime-free return to society.*

- *The bureau is a model of cost-efficient correctional operations and programs.*

- *A talented, professional, well-trained, and diverse staff reflect the bureau's culture and treat each other fairly.*

- *Staff work in an environment free from discrimination.*

- *A positive working relationship exists where employees maintain respect for one another.*

- *The workplace is safe, and staff perform their duties without fear of injury or assault.*

- *Staff are satisfied with their jobs, career opportunities, recognition, and quality of leadership.*

Making the Vision a Reality

This vision for an effective, safe, cost-efficient, fair, and just incarceration system for all those involved is appropriate and admirable. If realized, the incarceration system could be regarded as nothing less than a stunning success. But when one examines all the monetary, social, and moral costs still plaguing and resulting from the system, it is clear that the Federal Bureau of Prisons has far to

The main office of the Federal Bureau of Prisons is housed in the Federal Home Loan Bank Board Building in Washington, DC.

Although prison may seem too harsh a punishment in some cases, such as minor drug offenses, it is the only place to contain those who commit violent crimes.

go—particularly in the areas of public safety, inmate safety, and rehabilitative programming—before its vision is fully realized. Clearly, at least some reform is necessary.

In the United States today, a small, but healthy prison **abolition** movement is growing, This movement feels that America's extended social experiment with incarceration has gone on long enough, and its outcome is clear: incarceration does not reduce crime; it does not rehabilitate criminals; it does not address the real problems of poverty, lack of education, drug use, and mental illness; it does not make people safer; and it simply does not work.

Most people, however, would consider the prison abolition movement to be too **radical**. After all, regardless of the flaws in the U.S. incarceration system, it is holding more than 2.2 million people—people who cannot simply be released overnight back onto the street. For better or worse, incarceration is, at least at this time, an absolute necessity. Those who commit crimes and those who are dangerous to society must be held somewhere, and to date, no better system than the prison system has been developed to contain such criminals.

Voice of Experience

Does [the current incarceration system] represent "injustice or tyranny"? That depends on your point of view: If they are not going to be put to death, the monstrous . . . must be warehoused. Trying to extinguish the spark of the rest—the merely incorrigible, those holding on to civilization by a thread—itself feels like a monstrosity.

—TED CONOVER, *NEWJACK: GUARDING SING SING*

But does everyone who is currently in prison constitute a threat to society? Is everyone in prison being punished appropriately for their crimes? The declining crime rates of recent decades combined with **exponentially** increasing incarceration rates suggest no. Incarceration in the United States is being overly relied on with serious monetary, social, and moral costs.

Better Solutions Than Building More Prisons

At the present time, overcrowding is perhaps the number-one challenge standing in the way of meeting goals like the rehabilitation of prisoners, the assured safety of corrections workers, and the protection of inmates. Overcrowding, in turn, is due in greatest part to the **zealous** prosecution of drug offenders and mandatory sentencing laws. Many people, including those who work directly in the justice and incarceration systems (people like judges and prison administrators), are calling for the abolition of mandatory sentences. Repealing mandatory sentence legislation, however, may prove to be a tricky thing for politicians who don't wish to be labeled "soft on crime." Today, however, New York State, which was the country's leader in the drug war and harsh mandatory sentences, is now leading the way in repealing some of these laws. In the coming years, the state will serve as a good test case for whether getting rid of such laws improves the incarceration system.

Clearly, something must be done about the ever-increasing incarceration rates in the United States. The Bureau of Justice Statistics projects that an eventual 1 out of every 15 Americans will spend time in prison. No one could argue that such a figure would be a positive outcome of the present system. To stem the flow of people into prisons, changes will have to be made to the very economic, social, and political structures of the country—changes that address the poverty, lack of education, and drug culture that eventually send so many people to prison's gates.

Pushing for Prison Reform

President Obama advocates for prison reform.

Education Opportunity Can Turn Lives Around

Jamal's story exemplifies how providing youth in need with opportunities for education and advancement can turn their lives in completely new directions. Poor, black, struggling in school, living in a rural area, his father incarcerated, his mother deceased, no job experience, no money for college: according to all statistical models, Jamal had very little chance of "making it" in America. He was the **epitome** of a young person likely to get involved in crime and ultimately end up in jail.

But in Jamal's senior year of high school, something amazing happened. He learned about a foundation that provided full college scholarships for students in need. Unlike every other scholarship program Jamal had encountered, this full, four-year scholarship was completely need based. All the other scholarships Jamal had tried for were awarded to students who showed a combination of financial need and academic achievement. Jamal worked hard in school, but no matter how hard he worked, he just couldn't achieve the grades needed to get these academic scholarships. He thought there was no hope for him and college until he found this new scholarship program. He applied and was awarded the amazing gift. Suddenly, he was on his way to college, the first person in his family to ever pursue higher education.

While at college, Jamal has made the most of every opportunity presented to him. He is one of the school's top music students and is involved in one way or another in almost every musical production the small, liberal arts college puts on its stage. He became involved in theater and has been in charge of the lighting on numerous theatrical productions. He joined the Ultimate Frisbee team, and was able to travel to tournaments in several states. He has held jobs on and off campus, and throughout it all he has managed to maintain the grades necessary to keep his scholarship. This year he will graduate with a bachelor of arts degree.

Unfortunately, in America today, stories like Jamal's are few, and it will take a great deal of money and resources to transform the lives of the millions of youth who are presently at risk. Perhaps, if there is any hope of turning these lives around, it will mean investing government money, not in the building of new prisons, but in educational programs and social programs that have the potential to lift the nation's youth out of poverty and provide them with opportunities like the one Jamal was given.

In the end, the greatest cost of the incarceration system is the loss of a nation's youth. Currently, a great army of young people, mostly poor, black males, is marching, knowingly or unknowingly, down a road straight toward prison's gates. If they pass those gates, they will likely become like so many millions of others: lost potential, lost lives, and a nation's lost future.

Text-Dependent Questions

1. What are the three tenets of correctional service that the Federal Bureau of Prisons aims to embody?
2. Why do many politicians resist rolling back mandatory sentencing laws?
3. According to the Bureau of Justice Statistics, one in how many Americans may at one point have served time in prison?

Research Projects

1. Find a prison abolition organization. How did they start, and what are their specific, time-specific, long-term aims toward incarceration?
2. What sort of alternatives do prison-abolition groups advocate instead of incarceration?

Series Glossary

Abolition: The act of officially ending a law or practice.

Acquitted: Declared not guilty by a court or judge.

Adjudicated: Made a legal decision.

Advocacy: Active support for a cause or position.

Allegations: Statements saying someone has done something wrong or illegal.

Arbitrary: Based on whim or chance instead of logic.

Arson: The willful and malicious burning of property.

Asylum: Protection given by a government to someone who has left another country to escape being harmed.

At-risk: In danger of being harmed or damaged; in danger of failing or committing a crime.

Chronic: Something that is long term or recurs frequently.

Civil rights: Basic rights that all citizens of a society are supposed to have.

Coerce: Force someone to do something he or she does not want to do.

Community service: Unpaid work performed for the benefit of the local community that an offender is required to do instead of going to prison.

Constitutional freedoms: Rights to which every United states citizen is entitled as guaranteed by the Constitution. these include the right to free speech, to a free press, to practice one's religion, and to assemble peaceably.

Corporal punishment: Punishment that involves inflicting physical pain.

Court-martialed: Tried and convicted in a military court.

Defendant: In a criminal trial, the person accused of a crime.

Disposition: Settlement of a legal matter.

Detainees: People being detained, or kept in prison.

Disposition: Settlement of a legal matter.

Dissidents: Those who publicly disagree with an established political or religious system or organization.

Electronic monitoring: Electronic or telecommunications system, such as an ankle bracelet transmitter, used to track and supervise the location of an individual.

Exile: A punishment that forces a person to leave his or her country; also known as banishment.

Exonerated: Cleared of criminal charges or declared not guilty.

Extenuating circumstances: Reasons that excuse or justify someone's actions.

Extortion: The crime of obtaining something from someone using illegal methods of persuasion.

Extrajudicial: Outside normal legal proceedings.

Felonies: Serious crimes for which the punishment is usually imprisonment for more than a year.

Fraud: The crime of obtaining money or other benefit by the use of deliberate deception.

Grievance: A written complaint, delivered to authorities for resolution.

Halfway house: A residence for individuals after release from institutionalization (for a mental disorder, drug addiction, or criminal activity) that is designed to facilitate their readjustment to private life.

Hearing: Formal discussion of an inmates' case before a judge.

Humane: Having or displaying compassion.

Hunger strike: A refusal to eat, usually carried out by a prisoner as a form of protest.

Indicted: Formally charged someone with a crime.

Industrialized: Adapted to industrial methods of production and manufacturing.

Inherent: Innate or characteristic of something, and therefore unable to be considered separately.

Inhumane: Without compassion; cruel.

Inquest: A formal legal investigation.

Jurisdiction: A territory over which a government or agency has legal authority.

Larceny: The unlawful taking of personal property from another.

Lynching: Seizing someone believed to have committed a crime and putting him or her to death immediately and without trial, often by hanging.

Mandate: An order handed down by a governmental authority.

Misdemeanors: Minor crimes considered less serious than felonies.

Objective: Unbiased by personal feelings or interpretations.

Organized crime: Criminal activities that are widespread and centrally controlled like a business.

Parole: The early release of a prisoner with specified requirements, such as the need to report to authorities for a specified period.

Penology: The study of the treatment of criminals and incarceration.

Peremptory: Not open to debate or discussion.

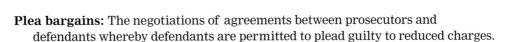

Plea bargains: The negotiations of agreements between prosecutors and defendants whereby defendants are permitted to plead guilty to reduced charges.

Precedent: An action or decision that can be used as an example for a later decision or to justify a similar action.

Probation: A period where an offender is released from prison but placed under supervision.

Protocols: Detailed rules and plans.

Psychotherapy: The treatment of mental illness through analysis or talk therapy.

Public-order crimes: Victimless crimes, such as prostitution.

Punitive: Inflicting or intended as punishment.

Quarantine: To separate to prevent contact.

Radical: Extreme.

Recidivism: The repeating of or returning to criminal behavior. The recidivism rate is the percentage of released prisoners who go on to commit new crimes.

Rehabilitation: To help someone return to good standing in the community.

Retribution: Punishment.

Repent: To express regret and seek forgiveness for past deeds, such as crimes.

Restitution: The act of making good or giving an equivalent for some injury.

Self-incrimination: The act of offering evidence or statements that would strongly suggest one's own guilt.

Shanks: Makeshift knives made out of other objects.

Sociopaths: People whose behavior is antisocial and who lack a conscience.

Status offender: A young person charged with an offense, such as running away from home or skipping school repeatedly, that would not be considered a crime if com- mitted by an adult.

Suspended sentences: Punishments that are not carried out so long as the person meets certain conditions.

Therapeutic: Helpful toward solving or curing a physical problem or illness.

Tribunal: A court or forum of justice.

Truancy: Being absent from school without an excuse.

Vagrancy: A lifestyle characterized by wandering with no permanent place to live.

Work-release program: A program that allows trusted offenders to work outside the correctional facility.

Workhouses: Publicly supported buildings where usually very poor people worked in exchange for housing and food.

Further Resources

Websites

Correctional Service of Canada: www.csc-scc.gc.ca

Death Penalty Information Center: www.deathpenaltyinfo.org

Here's Exactly What Our Addiction to Prison Costs You: http://www.attn.com/stories/2245/what-are-prisoners-costing-you

International Centre for Prison Studies: www.prisonstudies.org

New York Correction History Society: www.correctionhistory.org

The Drug War and Mass Incarceration by the Numbers: http://www.huffingtonpost.com/2013/04/08/drug-war-mass-incarceration_n_3034310.html

U.S. Bureau of justice Statistics: www.bjs.gov

U.S. Department of Justice: www.usdoj.gov

U.S. Federal Bureau of Prisons: www.bop.gov

Further Reading

Bruton, James H. *The Big House: Life Inside a Supermax Security Prison*. Stillwater, MN: Voyageur Press, 2004.

Conover, Ted. *Newjack: Guarding Sing Sing*. New York: Vintage Books, 2001.

Herivel, Tara, and Paul Wright, eds. *Prison Nation: The Warehousing of America's Poor*. New York: Routledge, 2003.

James, Joy, ed. *States of Confinement: Policing, Detention, and Prisons*. New York: Palgrave Macmillan, 2000.

Pollock, Joycelyn M. *Prisons and Prison Life: Costs and Consequences*. Los Angeles: Roxbury, 2004.

Williams, Stanley. *Life in Prison*. New York: Seastar Books, 2001.

Index

apartheid 19–20, 75

Canada 16, 19, 33, 37
Cannon, Joe Frank 63
capital punishment 10–11, 63, 75
Chomsky, Noam 62
Conover, Ted 32, 54, 56–57, 60, 72
corporal punishment 10–11, 75
Corrections Service of Canada 33
corrections workers 31, 36, 38, 54–55, 57, 72
crime rates 23, 49, 63, 72

death row 64
death sentence 10, 63, 64

education 14, 20, 22–23, 29, 47–48, 60–63, 67–68, 72–74
ethical challenges 11, 16

families 16, 29, 31–32, 38, 41, 44, 46–49, 54, 60–61
Federal Bureau of Prisons 16, 20, 23, 67–69
federal prisons 19–22, 33, 49, 54
freedom, loss of 11, 13

guards 57

health 29, 31–33, 46, 61, 68

hepatitis C 29, 33

incarceration rates 19–23, 49
incarceration system 9–11, 13, 16, 19, 24, 37, 41, 49, 57, 59–61, 68, 72–74

jails 10, 19–21, 30, 33, 41–42, 61, 73

laws 10, 49, 60, 72–73

medical care 27, 29, 32
monetary costs 16, 24, 27, 29, 38, 57, 68, 72
moral costs 16, 59–60, 68, 72

National Prison Association 11
Newjack: Guarding Sing Sing 54, 60, 72
North America 10–11, 16

penal system 10, 13, 20
poverty 20, 22–23, 60–63, 72–74
prison 9–11, 13–14, 16, 19–24, 27–34, 36–38, 41–44, 46–49, 53–57, 59–64, 67, 71–74
  costs of 16, 19, 27, 29, 31–33, 36, 37–38, 41, 47–48, 54–55, 57, 59–60
  effects of 29, 47
  evolution of 11
  goals of 67

overcrowding in 33–34, 36, 53, 72
race 20, 22
reform 11, 13, 49, 67, 72–73
types of 21, 23
women in 21, 46
prison abolition movement 72
prison industry 36
prison issues 9, 13
prisoner reform 11, 13, 49, 72
Prisons and Prison Life: Costs and Consequences 55–57
private prisons 36–37, 59, 67

Quakers 10

rehabilitation 13, 49, 59, 72
rules 9–10

Sing Sing 32, 54, 60–61, 72
social costs 13, 16, 38, 41, 47–49, 54, 57, 68, 72
social order 10, 13

tattoos 32–33
tuberculosis 29–30, 33

United States 9–11, 13, 19–21, 23, 27, 32–33, 36–37, 41, 49, 59–60, 63–64, 67, 72–73

war on drugs 51, 62–63
welfare 46, 60

About the Author

Autumn Libal earned her bachelor of arts from Smith College in Northampton, MA. She is the author of numerous educational books for young people. Other Mason Crest series she has written for include the European Union: Political, Social, and Economic Cooperation; Women's Issues: Global Trends; North American Indians Today; and Hispanic Heritage.

About the Series Consultant

Dr. Larry E. Sullivan is associate dean and chief librarian at the John Jay College of Criminal Justice and professor of criminal justice in the doctoral program at the Graduate School and University Center of the City University of New York. He first became involved in the criminal justice system when he worked at the Maryland Penitentiary in Baltimore in the late 1970s. That experience prompted him to write the book *The Prison Reform Movement: Forlorn Hope* (1990; revised edition 2002). His most recent publication is the book *The Brownsville Boys: Jewish Gangsters of Murder, Inc.* (2013). At John Jay College, in addition to directing the largest and best criminal justice library in the world, he teaches graduate and doctoral level courses in criminology and corrections. John Jay is the only liberal arts college with a criminal justice focus in the United States and is internationally recognized as a leader in criminal justice education, research, and training.

Picture Credits